Ant Farms
for Beginners

ALINA DARIA

Contents

Introduction

Small but mighty! Ants may be tiny animals - but they are nevertheless fascinating creatures that exhibit extremely interesting social structures and characteristics. This is why people have been interested in ants for a long time. However, for the longest time observations mainly took place in the wild or in research.

Slowly, ants are establishing themselves as extremely popular pets - both for adults and children. Of course, they are not "cuddly animals" like dogs and cats, but animals for observation. When the ants are busy, some people spend quite a lot of time in front of the formicarium, because when observing them, one tends to forget the time and ignores their traditional TV.

But even though ants are extremely small, they are important creatures that need to be respected and treated well. Therefore, it is essential to learn about the needs of these industrious creatures before purchasing them to ensure that you can offer them a nice and species-appropriate home.

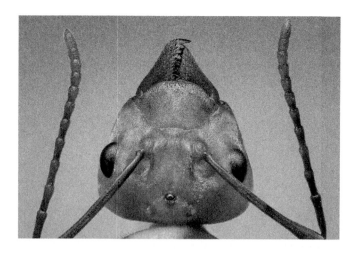

© Ronny Overhate

Family, Genera and Species

As every child probably already knows, ants belong to the insects. Within the insect class, ants belong to the order of the so-called *Hymenoptera*. What is generally less known, however, is that ants belong to the suborder *Apocrita* - and these are wasps.

The scientific name of the ant family is *Formicidae*. The name was introduced in 1802 by the French entomologist Pierre André Latreille (1762-1833). Entomologists are insect researchers. From the scientific name of the ants is also derived the name of their "special terrarium" - formicarium.

FORMICIDAE

So far, so good. *Formicidae* is a family in the animal kingdom - and it is with this family that we will be taking a closer look in this book. But this is by no means the end of the story! Within the family, animals are also divided into genera and then into species.

The genera are one rank below the families in the hierarchy. Usually, several species belong to one genus. However, it is also possible that only one species belongs to a genus - then the genus is called 'monotypic'.

Each species has a two-part scientific name. The first part of the name is the genus to which the species belongs, and the second part of the name is the species epithet. An epithet is simply a suffix.

For example, quite popular genera are the following:

- Genus Camponotus

- Genus Lasius

- Genus Myrmica

- Genus Formica

- Genus Aphaenogaster

As a rule, the ants of these genera are also well suited for beginners. The following species are particularly suitable for beginners ...

... Formica fusca

... Formica rufibarbis

... Lasius flavus

... Lasius niger

© CP17

Which Ant Species Should I Choose?

Not all ants are the same! The different species are sometimes very different and do not always have the same requirements in terms of ambient temperature, etc.

The needs of some species are more difficult to satisfy than the needs of other species - therefore there are some species that are comparatively rather easy to care for and have therefore established themselves as "beginner species".

Easy to keep species should not have complicated requirements for humidity in the formicarium and for their ambient temperature. They should be able to tolerate small fluctuations well and not die quickly in case of minor mistakes. Furthermore, the growth of the colony should be neither too fast nor too slow. Too fast growth can easily overwhelm a beginner, but too slow growth can also raise doubts as to whether the housing conditions may be wrong.

Some species have a poisonous sting, but in most cases this is harmless. Contrary to the common belief that some ant species bite, this is not the case: they mostly sting! The stings are often mistaken for bites. Usually these stings are harmless, but if there are already known allergies to other insects, you are well advised not to choose ant species with venomous stings ("defence stings"). Ants that have a sting include the Ponerinae and the Myrmicinae.

The secretion secreted from the sting is similar to the venom of wasps and bees. If you are allergic to wasp or bee stings, for example, you should always choose a stingless species.

Furthermore, it is a good idea for beginners not to choose ants that are too small. Firstly, it is much easier to pick up a slightly larger ant with your finger in case it falls down or needs to be picked up for some other reason. The smaller the species, the higher the chance of unintentionally hurting the ant - especially if you are still a little careless. Secondly, all ants are very good at escaping and need good escape protection, which must be checked regularly so that the ants do not accidentally spread around the home. Of course, the smaller ants are, the more difficult it is to keep them under control. Very small species include, for example, Solenopsis fugax (which belong to the fire ants) or Temnothorax.

It is also important to mention that some ant species go into hibernation and other species do not. This is a point not to be neglected - some keepers do not want them to hibernate and therefore choose species that do not hibernate naturally.

We have already listed some examples of different species that beginners can usually keep quite well and successfully. Of course, opinions differ on this as well and not everyone makes the division between difficult/medium/easy in the same way. Nevertheless, it can be said that the species we will look at in a little more detail below have established themselves as quite beginner friendly.

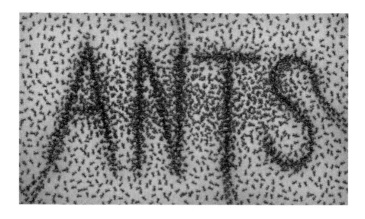

© *James Jimmy Larkin*

... Formica fusca

The ants of this species are medium-sized, and the colony develops rather quickly. The bodies are black and quite shiny. The queen of this species usually has a body size of about 0.4 inches, while the workers grow to about 0.2 to 0.3 inches. The colonies of this species remain comparatively small and usually have between 400 and 2,000 workers. This also depends on how many queens there are; some colonies of this species have only one queen, others may even have about a dozen queens.

... Formica rufibarbis

This species is very active and therefore makes great animals for observation. The size of the ants is quite moderate at about 0.2 inches; the ants are not too small but can still be observed well. To do well, they also need warmth and sufficient nutrients, of course, but in general they are comparatively undemanding and frugal animals. This species goes into hibernation.

... Lasius flavus

This species should also hibernate. It is a species that can be found very often in Europe and lives in nature on meadows. The size can be placed in the middle range, whereby the workers are quite small with a length of 0.07 to 0.15 inches. The males are usually a little larger and the queen is about 0.35 inches long. The yellow colouration of this species is striking.

... Lasius niger

This species is extremely popular in the home formicarium, and many beginners start with a colony of Lasius niger. The good reputation and popularity are not unusual, because this species is actually one of the least squeamish species among the ants. Of course, you should also take good care of Lasius niger and make sure that they are always nice and warm, that they get enough protein, etc. - but beginner's mistakes are usually not fatal, because this species is very adaptable and does not die quickly. Other plus points for Lasius niger are that the species is very active and therefore great to watch, on the one hand, and very cheap to buy, on the other. It should be noted, however, that the species should be able to hibernate in any case.

Lasius Niger – © Sandeep Handa

... Myrmica rubra

This species has a defensive sting and is therefore not suitable for people who have already shown allergic reactions to wasp stings, for example. It cannot be ruled out that the ants will also sting humans, so no risk should be taken here. Apart from that, Myrmica rubra is a great ant species for beginners, as they are also quite robust. What is important is sufficient warmth and humidity. This species also goes into hibernation.

... Aphaenogaster senilis

This ant species is very suitable for beginners, because although it depends on warmth to grow and live well and healthy, it is not very sensitive. With this species, the ants should be offered a lot more proteins, among other things because this ant species lays its larvae on the proteins - that is, on dead insects that the keeper makes available to them. The larvae are very dependent on this high supply of protein. This species also goes into hibernation.

... Camponotus nicobarensis

This species is an exotic species that has become quite popular - both with beginners and experienced ant keepers. As a rule, they are therefore somewhat more expensive. The species is not particularly squeamish, but rather robust. Of course, they also need warmth and sufficient nutrients, but compared to other species they are rather insensitive. This species does not usually hibernate.

... Camponotus vagus

This species also needs enough warmth, but in contrast to the above-mentioned species it hibernates. If the hibernation does not disturb the keeper, these ants are great observers, because they grow very large - the queen and some workers often even measure more than 0.4 inches. The larvae reach their size quite quickly, because the development from egg to larva to adult worker takes only about one and a half months.

© *Sathish Kumar*

Getting the Ants

The procurement of ants is somewhat different from that of other pets. "Ordinary" pets such as dogs, cats, rabbits and the like can be adopted from an animal shelter, obtained from a foster home, bought from a breeder, and so on. With ants, the situation is somewhat different.

The best thing is to raise your own colony from the beginning. It is fascinating to watch how the ant colony develops and how slowly an organisation and a structure are formed within the colony. This is also usually better for the ants, as the colony develops and regulates itself in a natural way. If, for example, you only take over parts of a colony - often from nature - you cannot be sure that you have got the whole colony and imbalances may arise in the colony which, in the worst case, can become so serious that the colony perishes.

First of all, you should decide what kind of ants you want to keep. The species should not be mixed with another species. It is easiest to keep a species of ant that is native to your region. However, descriptions such as "European" or "exotic" are only of limited help, because Europe, for example, is large and has very different climate zones. Even on the northern American continent, the climate zones are quite different - while it gets bitterly cold in winter in some US states, in other states you look in vain for snow in winter. Therefore, it is advisable to narrow down the region in which the respective species occurs as much as possible. As mentioned before, choosing a native species - i.e., one that occurs in the region where you live - is usually the easiest, as the temperatures and humidity do not need to be regulated to any great extent.

Nevertheless, it is of course also possible to raise and keep ants that are native to another climate zone - in this case, however, you have to pay more attention to the respective climate and, for example, heat the formicarium if necessary, ensure higher humidity, etc.

You can either collect the ant(s) yourself in the wild or buy them from a breeder or similar. Collecting a native species is not as difficult as you might think - if you know what to look for and when to do it. If you collect a fertilised young queen, you can use her to raise a new colony at home. For this, of course, the young queen must have been mated beforehand.

In most cases, queens are quite easy to recognise, as they are usually larger than the rest of the ants. If the queen still has her wings, however, it can be assumed that she has not yet been mated. After the nuptial flight and after the young queen has been mated, she sheds her wings relatively quickly and starts "egg production" to establish her colony. The greatest thing is therefore to find a young queen that has already been mated but has not yet started colony growth. However, it must be mentioned that even unfertilised queens can shed their wings - there is no hundred percent guarantee, and you may need several attempts.

The young queen should first be allowed to start the colony in a test tube or similar container/nest and only be moved to the "real" formicarium when a small colony has already developed.

If you do not want to collect the ants yourself, but buy them from a breeder, you can also either just buy a mated young queen or buy the queen together with some eggs and/or workers. However, the ants should not be mixed wildly, but the eggs and/or the workers should clearly come from the selected queen, so that there are no problems later; for example, because the queen does not accept the workers. There also "tolerant queens" that accept workers from another colony or from another queen, but there is no guarantee for this either.

The annual rhythm of an ant and when reproduction takes place usually varies somewhat from species to species, but in general it can be said that most ant colonies produce new young queens in the summer months, i.e., have their mating season in summer. If these queens no longer have wings, they have most likely already been mated and can be taken away. Collecting a few young queens will not disturb nature or upset the balance in the animal kingdom.

However, whether and how much success you have with the queen is still a matter of luck to a certain extent, because there is no guarantee of successful reproduction and colony growth. Many people try it with a single queen first, other people try it with three or four different queens straight away. However, one should refrain from collecting even more queens, because in the event that all of them are actually able to establish a successful colony, you will end up with masses of ants that you will have to house or give away.

© *Federico Maderno*

Furthermore, one should also refrain from searching for the queen in existing nests in order to "steal" her. It is very likely that you will not find the queen anyway and instead only destroy the nest that the ants have diligently built. And even if you find the queen, this will most likely mean the death of the entire ant colony. Therefore, you should only take young queens that you can easily find and do not have to search in the nest.

Furthermore, ants that are not native to the respective region should never be released into the wild. In some countries this is even illegal.

Ants have relatively fixed periods of the year when they mate - for most species this is around the summer months. This is when the so-called nuptial flights take place.

The nuptial flights usually take place when it is nice and warm and windless, and it shouldn't be too rainy either. The sexually mature males and the young queens swarm out - with the sole aim of mating. Apart from that, the ants have no business flying in the air. Therefore, the ants only use their wings for the nuptial flight; after successful mating, the wings are thrown off or bitten off. These ants are the so-called "reproductive animals" - i.e., the young queens that are to be mated and the males whose sole task in life is to mate with the young queens.

It is particularly interesting that the young queens do not mate with just one male, but with several at once. The collected sperm are then stored by the queen in her body and these collected sperm must suffice forever. Later, no more mating takes place, but the queen always falls back on the sperm stored in her body after her maiden flight. And when you consider that, depending on the species, a queen can sometimes live for over twenty years, that's quite a considerable supply!

The males, meanwhile, wait patiently in the nest until it is time for the nuptial flight, then fulfil their task and die a little later - a rather uninteresting life.

If collecting a young queen yourself is not desired or not possible, it can also be bought. Often young queens are sold with a few eggs and/or larvae, so you can be sure that the queen has already been fertilised. Some breeders/vendors already start to raise the colony slowly in order to sell it as a whole. Nevertheless, you should always pay attention to the seriousness of the supplier, otherwise this can lead to disappointment if the colony does not develop properly or even dies.

As explained before, the young queen is usually initially kept in a test tube or similar container until the first workers have developed. Once the colony is past the initial stage, it can be moved to the formicarium. People usually keep queen ants in test tubes because the confined test tube simulates a kind of underground chamber for a newly mated young queen. This form of accommodation usually induces them to lay their fertilised eggs.

In the test tube, the lower part of the container is sealed with cotton wool or a piece of tampon so that water is stored at one end of the test tube. This water, sealed in here, will supply the young queen with water/humidity as she lays her eggs and the colony slowly takes shape. This usually takes a few weeks. Exactly how long this takes varies somewhat between species and also depends on how warm it is. Most species take about two weeks for an egg to develop into a larva and then into a worker.

For good growth and development, it is important that the nutrient supply, temperature and humidity are suitable. The test tube should also not be exposed to bright light - let alone direct sunlight, because direct sunlight is not only too bright, but can also quickly heat up the temperature in the test tube so that everything dies. Therefore, the test tube should be kept in a fairly dark place and you should also not disturb the queen too much, for example by moving it. However, care should be taken that no mould forms in the test tube due to the water and that the water does not dry out -

then the young queen with her eggs/larvae must be relocated to a new test tube. The queen in the test tube does not need to be fed, as she feeds on her flight muscles anyway, which are no longer needed, and often also on other stored reserves.

As already mentioned, the non-existent wings are an indication that the queen has already mated - but there is no guarantee for this. There are ants that do not break off their wings even after mating and sometimes keep them for a long time, even if they have already been mated. Therefore, broken wings are only one sign.

Another quite clear sign of successful mating is a thick, bloated gaster. This is the abdomen of the queen or the abdomen of ants in general, where most of the organs are located. If the gaster is bloated as a result of mating, this is called "physogastry". However, it must be mentioned that workers can also get into a physogastric state, for example if they have taken in a lot of fluid. A third sign that a queen has been mated is that she intensively cleans her gaster.

© *Egor Kamelev Ekamelev*

Anatomy

The body structure of ants differs significantly from the body structure of our more "established" domestic animals and should therefore be known at least roughly in order to better understand the ant and its body functions. It is particularly striking that the ant's body is very clearly divided into three parts: the caput, the thorax and the gaster. This is the head of the ant, in the middle of the body is the thoracic area and the gaster is the abdomen of the animal. Therefore, let us take a closer look at each of the body parts and senses below.

Eyes:

While humans are most dependent on their eyes for perception and orientation, the eyes of most ants do not fulfil any essential tasks. They are rather poorly developed and are mainly used to see how bright or dark it is. In addition, they also perceive environmental movements. There are species that have better developed eyes, but this is the exception rather than the rule. Most ant species therefore rely much more on their antennae than on their eyes.

Antennae:

Ants' antennae are by far their most important sensory organ. The antennae are multifunctional, because with them the ant can not only perceive scents and tastes, but also very small temperature fluctuations as well as vibrations, air currents and oscillations. The antennae are therefore not classic sensory organs as in mammals, for example, but fulfil many different functions, from feeling and orientation to smelling. The fact that the ant can also perceive such fine temperature fluctuations and small air currents shows how sensitive and important the antennae are.

Sensory hairs:

Ants do not have classic ears and therefore no hearing like mammals, for example. However, this does not mean that they are completely indifferent to sounds - they do sense the waves that are created by sounds. When we listen to music, for example, we not only perceive what we hear, but also the sound waves and bass that are created by this music. This is also the case with ants, because they can perceive these sound waves through very fine sensory hairs that are all over their bodies.

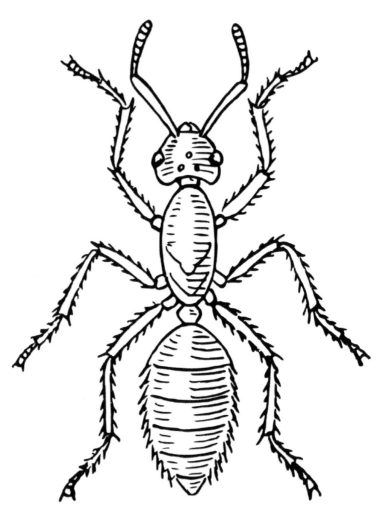

© Open Clipart Vectors

Mandibles:

The mandibles are the typical mouthparts of ants. The mandibles are used in many different ways, depending on the species. For example, ants can crush and bite food with their mandibles. They are also very useful for transporting objects, for example food or nesting material. There are also some species that can cut leaves and other material with their mandibles. In predatory species, it further happens that the mouthparts are also used to attack the prey.

Legs:

Ants have six legs. The legs are located on the middle part of the body, i.e. the thorax. There are three pairs of legs. These legs also consist of six limbs: the claw limb (at the bottom), the foot, the splint, the thigh, the thigh ring and the hip limb.

Thorax:

The thorax is the middle part of the ant's body, i.e. the thoracic part. However, it is also divided into three parts: the prothorax, the mesothorax and the metathorax. The metathorax is the rearmost part, where there is a segment that connects the thorax to the gaster. This segment is called the "epinotum".

Alitrunk:

The alitrunk is the part of an insect's body where the wings are located. The problem with ants, however, is that not all ants have wings - only males and the young queens that have not yet been mated have wings, because the only function of wings in ants is to carry out the nuptial flight during which mating takes place. After mating, the young queens no longer need their wings and therefore get rid of them. The males die shortly after mating anyway, as the only function of the males is to fertilise the young queens. Therefore, only some ants have wings; and not permanently, but only for a short time. Therefore, strictly speaking, the thorax of ants cannot be called alitrunk, since the wings are precisely absent in most cases or are only present for a short time.

Petiolus/Postpetiolus:

In entomology, this is the term for the area of the "narrow waist" in ants and some other insects. This consists of either one segment or two segments. The second stalk limb is therefore called the postpetiolus (post = after). These parts are jointed and not rigid, so the gaster can move well in different directions.

Gaster:

The gaster is the rear part of the ant's body. Almost all the ant's organs are located in the gaster, e.g., the important crop (social stomach), and in many species also a venom sting. Due to its flexibility, this venom spine or the defence spine can be moved in different directions. The gaster is also very expandable, which is helpful when, for example, a lot of food is ingested.

Crop:

The crop is the social stomach of the ant. It is extremely important for ants because a worker can "store" food in her crop and regurgitate it as needed.

In this way, she transports a lot of food from A to B and can supply the queen as well as larvae and possibly other workers with food by regurgitating it. This also explains why the crop is called a "social stomach" - because it not only serves to feed the receiving ant, but also serves to feed other colony members.

Forestomach/proventriculus:

The forestomach regulates the transfer of food from the crop to the midgut, because of course the crop is not only for feeding other colony members, but also for feeding the receiving ant itself. The exact structure of the forestomach varies from species to species. The forestomach then leads into the midgut.

Glands:

The glands are very important for ants as they release scents through them and communicate in many ways through these scents. This special type of scent is called "pheromones". By means of their pheromones, ants can send different signals to their conspecifics and recruit them. For example, if an ant has found food and needs the help of other ants, it can use pheromones to get them to come along and lay a scent trail that the other ants can follow and thus also find the target.

In many cases, pheromones are also used to ward off enemies, because a colony has a unique nest scent, which can be used to identify and ward off enemies. However, this does not always work, or does not work for all species.

So, there is not just one ultimate pheromone that ants use to communicate and regulate, but many different ones. For example, there are pheromones that are emitted by the queen to regulate the fertility of her workers. These pheromones ensure that the workers do not lay eggs, as this task is reserved for the queen. Nevertheless, it can happen from time to time that workers lay eggs - but these are usually then used as food.

In addition, there are pheromones that are secreted especially by the larvae to signal that they need food.

The glands are located all over the body; many are secreted specifically from the gaster, but there are also many glands all over the body that can also secrete pheromones.

Genitalia:

The male ants, whose sole function is to fertilise the young queens and who die shortly afterwards, have two testes and associated vas deferens. The females have two ovaries, but usually only the queen is fertile. The ovaries of the workers are in many cases atrophied (or non-existent) and, in addition, the queen also emits pheromones that are supposed to "sterilise" the workers so that they do not reproduce or lay eggs. As mentioned before, this does not always work, and it can happen that a worker lays eggs. These are then usually used as food. In the unlikely event that larvae or ants do develop from these eggs, they will be males because the worker's eggs were unfertilised - and unfertilised eggs always develop into males in ants.

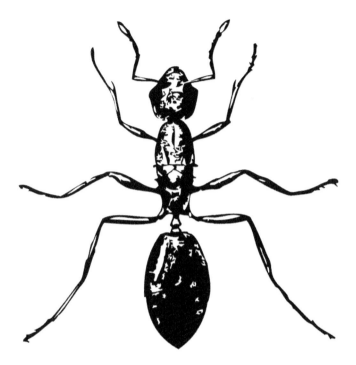

© Clker Free Vector Images

The Different Roles in the Colony

In an ant colony, each ant performs a specific task - no ant is useless. It is fascinating to watch how the ants form their colony and how they establish an organisation within this colony. Teamwork is very important to ants.

One of the most interesting aspects about ants is the fact that the males are not assigned an important role in the colony - well, they have a single important task, but after completing this their existence is superfluous and they die after a short time.

The males - unlike the females - develop from unfertilised eggs. While female ants often live for several years, the male ants often only live for a few weeks. Their only task is to reproduce and thus ensure the further development of the colony, because their existence is based on the fact that they mate with a (young) queen during the so-called nuptial flight and thus ensure the continuity of the female ants. Once this task is fulfilled, the males usually die quite quickly. They do not become an important part of the organisation within the colony, but only serve to maintain and further reproduce the colony.

Within the female ants, a distinction is made between the queens and the workers. Not every colony has only one queen; a colony can also have several queens, depending on the species and size. But in every colony, it is true that there are many more workers than queens. The queen - similar to the males - also has only one task, which she does, however, not only once, but over and over again: she produces eggs and thereby ensures that the colony is enlarged and strengthened. It is therefore the sole task of the queen or queens to take care of the offspring. As a rule, queens also live very long - compared to workers. Of course, this also differs depending on the species and living conditions. However, specimens have been known to live 20 years and more. Unfortunately, the workers do not have such a long life as the queens.

The workers, as mentioned before, form the largest group within the colony. While the queens are only responsible for producing new ant offspring, the workers are responsible for everything else - except laying eggs. The workers are very industrious animals, because they take care of the provision of water and food, they look after the brood, they build the nest, they defend their nest and they care for and look after the queens.

Nevertheless, the workers are of course still females, so it is theoretically - and sometimes in practice - possible for workers to lay eggs as well but this rarely happens. However, if a worker does lay eggs, these eggs are often used as food. This can happen, for example, when there is an imbalance in the colony and tasks are no longer clearly allocated - most often this is the case when a queen has died and therefore there is no longer an orderly structure as before. In the unlikely event that a worker's eggs are not eaten but do develop, male ants will emerge. As we have learned before, males only develop from unfertilised eggs - and this is the case with worker ants' eggs.

The queens are usually quite easy to distinguish from the workers because they are larger. Especially the middle part of the queen's body is significantly larger than that of the workers - this part is called the thorax. In addition, queens have large ovaries. These factors ensure that the body of a queen is in almost all cases significantly larger than the body of a worker.

However, not all workers are the same. In many ant species there are further subdivisions within the worker group and the ants are assigned certain tasks. This is not always the case, but in many species such structures can be identified, making the organisation and structure within the colony even more efficient.

The workers differ in size - the smallest are often called Minor/Minore and the largest ants are called Major/Majore. In addition, there are often ants that are in between the majors and minors in terms of size; these are called media. But probably the most interesting are the soldiers - these special workers do a very special job, because the soldiers defend their colony against intruders and other dangers. However, depending on the species, the soldiers are often given other tasks; for example, they are often responsible for crushing particularly hard food (e.g. hard fig seeds) or they are supposed to transport particularly large and/or heavy objects, such as especially large food that cannot be easily broken up, into the nest.

There are also some species that act like bouncers in front of their nest! For example, in Camponotus truncatus, the soldiers guard the entrances to their colony's nest. In case of danger, the soldiers close these entrances and thus protect their colony.

How exactly individual ants become the special soldiers has long been unclear and often considered mysterious. In 2018, it was discovered at McGill University in Canada that a seemingly irrelevant "organ" regulates this division. The colony itself produces these female soldiers and this "organ" is developed very late; in the last stage of larval development. Only the ants that subsequently become soldiers develop this "organ". This is the rudimentary wing discs.

Previously, it was assumed that this development occurs due to different hormonal stages or is influenced by nutrition. However, it has now been discovered that this separates the female soldiers from the "normal workers". They grow bigger and faster and often develop huge mandibles, for example. Mandibles are the mouthparts of ants and other insects.

© *Egor Kamelev Ekamelev*

In addition, the McGill University researchers (Rajakumar, Abouheif et al.) found that the colony itself maintains the natural balance between normal workers and soldiers by regulating the growth of the larvae's vestigial wing discs. If the ants find that there are too many female soldiers, the growth of the vestigial wing discs is stopped with a growth-inhibiting pheromone. In this way, the colony can regulate the number of female soldiers, which in most cases amounts to about 5 to 10 percent of the total colony.

Since the rudimentary wing discs only develop in the last stage of larval development, the ants are also able to increase the number of their female soldiers quite quickly when they notice that there is increased danger and that the colony now needs more female soldiers. With these results, the McGill University researchers found answers to questions that even Charles Darwin was already pondering at the time!

The Formicarium

The ant farm, the formicarium, the arena, the nest, ... What is all this and what are the differences? While some terms relating to ant keeping are very familiar, you are probably less familiar with other terms and are confronted with them for the first time when researching ants.

A formicarium is used specifically for keeping ants. While the word "terrarium", for example, is commonly known because it is so often used for keeping reptiles and also for keeping snails and the like, the word "formicarium" is less familiar.

If one knows the Latin terms and/or the scientific name of ants, the term can be derived very easily. The

Latin word for "ant" is "formica" - and we have already learned the scientific name of the ant family ("formicidae"). The suffix "-arium" is used for premises or collections, as with the terms aquarium, terrarium, etc.

The formicarium is therefore the entire ant home. This is often a converted terrarium/aquarium, but not always. Formicariums can differ in type and form and do not always have to consist of only one room, but the rooms can also be connected with each other. For example, many keepers have separated the nest and the arena and connected the two spaces. It is important that the ants have access to all areas of the formicarium. Some ant keepers also do not have just one arena for their ants, but several arenas, but they are always connected and allow the ants access.

Although ants are generally quite robust animals, they should still have their peace and quiet to a large extent so that they are not exposed to too much stress. It is therefore important to think carefully in advance about where the formicarium can be placed. There are four points to consider in particular:

1. Noise: it does not have to be as quiet as a mouse around the formicarium; everyday noises are perfectly fine and do not harm the animals. However, the ants should not be bothered by too much noise. It is therefore better not to place the formicarium directly next to the television or a music system.

2. Possible shocks or vibrations: Excessive vibrations should also be avoided as far as possible. A place under the stairs is therefore usually not ideal. In addition, it should be noted that loudness can of course also cause vibrations - a music system with booming bass is not only loud, but also causes sometimes huge vibrations.

3. The movements in front of the formicarium: In addition, the formicarium should be placed in a rather quiet corner, where adults, children and possibly even

other pets do not constantly walk past. The corridor of a flat is therefore usually less suitable.

4. Sunlight: Ants depend on humidity in the formicarium in order not to dry out - because ants can die quite quickly from dehydration. It is therefore important that the formicarium is always kept moist (not wet!). Direct sunlight would dry out the formicarium quite quickly. In addition, direct sunlight can also lead to a rapid rise in temperature.

It is best to choose a material as substrate for the formicarium that is also the substrate for the ants in nature: As a rule, this is conventional organic potting soil. Some ant keepers also use coarse-grained sand or fine gravel. However, the size of the ants should also be considered. Small species, for example, may have problems moving on coarse sand or pebbles. Organic soil, on the other hand, is suitable for all species.

Another option for a fairly natural substrate is a mixture of clay and sand. Mixing it with clay makes the substrate loose and still very natural, but the soil gives the ants a better grip when walking than if only sand were used. Depending on the mixing ratio, the consistency then resembles that of conventional soil. Depending on the species, a harder or looser substrate can be created by changing the ratio. But no matter which substrate you choose - the soil, clay and/or sand should always be of organic quality and thus free of pesticides and other pollutants.

Ants not only like a moist environment, but also a functional one. Therefore, they don't care what decorative objects or pretty plants are in their formicarium - because they will only examine the objects for functionality and see what can be used well for nest building. Of course, it's great if the formicarium also houses a few plants, because plants always contribute to a pleasant climate and create a natural habitat. They are also important for air quality and humidity. On the other hand, there are also many keepers who do without plants in the formicarium altogether, for example to prevent mites from multiplying too much.

Nevertheless, too expensive or sensitive plants should be avoided, because the ants like to use pieces of plants or - depending on the size - even the entire plant to build their nest. Succulents are therefore quite suitable because they are robust and easy to care for. It is also a good idea to use plants with only a few roots or no roots at all to minimise the risk of the ants burrowing in. Ficus pumila or Oxalis acetosella are also very suitable for a formicarium. The plants should not need too much water to avoid too much water accumulation, which could be dangerous for the ants.

Ants usually build their nests either on the ground or in wood - or they are opportunistic nest builders. Opportunists are not dependent on a certain material or on a certain place but settle where it is possible and where they can meet their needs for food and moisture - but of course this place must also offer protection.

© Sergio Cerrato Italia

Nevertheless, most species are ants that nest on/in the ground. How exactly the nest is built and what it finally looks like also varies from species to species. Some nests are quite simple, for example with a vertical tunnel and branches on the tunnel sides where eggs, larvae, food etc. are placed. Some nests, however, are more intricately built, extending quite far and with many underground passages and tunnels that create a fascinating network of pathways.

Other species, however, for example Camponotus spp. nest in damp wood such as dead wood pieces, which, however, do not dry out but are rotten or otherwise damp. Such species also like to nest in tree trunks or sometimes in the branches of trees. There are even some species that use tree leaves to build their nests.

© *Julio CB*

An ant farm is intended to "replace" the naturally occurring earth nest for the ants and give them the opportunity to build a species-appropriate nest - similar to the way they would do it in nature. The ants are provided with a lot of soil substrate with which they can build their tunnels and chambers in the same way as they would in the wild. Through glass or Plexiglas panes, the activities of the ants can be observed quite well and can be very fascinating, as the ants actually build very complex and sophisticated systems, depending on the species.

In common parlance, the term "ant farm" is often used for the entire formicarium or home of the ants. Strictly speaking, however, the ant farm is only the part of the formicarium that the ants use for nest building. The so-called "arena", in which the ants forage, is to be distinguished from this. Arena? Forage? What does this mean again?

The term "arena" sounds spectacular at first, but simply put, it is nothing more than the area of the formicarium that the ants use for the rest of their activities - for example, to collect food. As we already know, formicariums can look very different and simply represent the entirety of the space that the ants have at their disposal and are allowed to access - regardless of whether the formicarium is built in a classic terrarium or a complex system consisting of several containers. In the meantime, there are also some suppliers who offer special nest containers, arena containers, etc., which can be connected with each other as required.

"Forage" is simply the name for the gathering of food by the workers. The word originates from French and is based on the term "fourrage", which is used to describe animal feed.

In the past, this word was also often used in the military, for example when fodder was collected for horses or other animals. Nowadays it is most common among insect keepers and refers to the organisation of food. In ants, it is specifically the workers who forage; the queens do not bother with foraging.

Foraging takes place in the arena. The arena should be as close as possible to the natural habitat of the ant species and resemble the environment in the wild. What exactly this environment looks like naturally varies somewhat from species to species.

In the arena, the ant workers look for food and water. The food and water should always be placed in the arena and not directly in/at the nest - the workers take care of transporting the food themselves. The food can simply be placed in the arena without a food bowl. There are even special water bottles for ants; sometimes birdbaths are used if they are constructed safely and if it is not possible for the ants to drown.

While care should be taken that the nest is always moist (not wet!) enough, this is negligible for the arena. The arena is only for foraging and not for "living and growing up" like the nest. However, the arena should not dry out either.

In addition, the ants also deposit their waste in the arena. However, they do not scatter it indiscriminately in the arena, but are quite orderly and usually create a rubbish heap where they deposit everything they cannot use. On this pile, the ants collect their droppings, dead ants, food remains that are no longer needed, and the like. The waste heap should not be too close to the nest so that the nest is not contaminated. Furthermore, this area should be cleaned regularly by the ant keeper. The ants make it very easy for us humans, as they do not spread their waste everywhere, but are very clean animals and keep their waste collected. Therefore, the waste can be removed very easily.

Some keepers even integrate a separate waste container into their formicarium - the ants are thus provided with a separate small container just for collecting waste. This is not absolutely necessary, but it does emphasise the cleanliness of the ants' home. However, the ants must of course be taught what this separate container is for - because the ants will build their rubbish heap where they consider it right and sensible. You cannot force them to put their rubbish somewhere else. But if you regularly take the rubbish heap and do not dispose of it immediately, but relocate it - i.e., place it in the separate container - there is a good chance that the ants will accept this new place and store their rubbish there from now on. Of course, there is no guarantee. It is also important that this separate container is not used for anything other than waste disposal.

The nest should be kept moist, but accumulations of too much water should be avoided. In the worst case, chambers and tunnels can be flooded and the ants could even drown. Light humidification can easily be achieved with a spray bottle, for example, which sprays fine water vapour over a wide area. Due to the humidity, however, sufficient ventilation should be ensured, otherwise there is a risk that mould will form due to the accumulated humidity, that mites will proliferate, and so on. If the nest and the arena are not in the same room, but are connected to each other, the connecting pieces should be at least large enough to allow the ants to pass each other comfortably in opposite directions and to prevent congestion.

© *Franco Patrizia*

However, not all ant species have their nest separate from their arena. If the nest is integrated into the arena, one speaks - as can already be assumed - of an integrated nest. It is also not necessary for the ants to have only one arena available - they are also happy to have several arenas. These, for example, be connected to each other by connectors and be located in different containers. This way the ants also have a bit more variety and get the feeling that they can explore more and that their habitat is larger - which is true! How many arenas the ants should have at their disposal depends, of course, on how much space the keeper wants to/can provide.

On the subject of "nests", a special type should also be mentioned: the Ytong nest - or also called an aerated concrete nest. Ytong is in fact simply a very well-known brand.

This nest is very popular, among other things because it is very easy to observe what the ants are up to and how hard they work. This nest is a ready-built nest that the ants cannot/do not have to build themselves. However, it is still possible to fill the prefabricated tunnels with soil substrate, for example, so that the ants can still have an influence on the nest design. Depending on the material, there are sometimes even such strong ants that they can even work the aerated concrete. However, this applies to only a few species.

The Ytong/porous concrete nest can either be bought ready-made - i.e., with prefabricated tunnels - or you can make it yourself. The advantage of aerated concrete/Ytong is also that the material soaks through. Therefore, there is no danger of the nest drying out because moisture can get inside. Humidification options here include a humidification pit or backwater under the nest.

One of the most important points in ant keeping and at the same time one of the most frequently discussed topics is the correct and effective escape protection - because on the one hand no one wants to have ants running around freely in the house and on the other hand you are not doing the ants any favours if they escape, either. There are several options for escape protection, some of which can be combined with each other. Which forms of escape protection are suitable and recommended for the respective ant species can also differ somewhat - for example, some species cannot run up glass walls and therefore escape protection with oil/grease is not necessary. Other species, on the other hand, cannot even be stopped by oil/grease; again, such escape protection would not be effective. Which escape protection is effective for the desired species should therefore be found out in advance or asked of the breeder/seller. Some examples:

1. Talcum powder: For example, conventional baby powder is suitable as talcum powder. As a breakout protection, a two- to three-centimetre-thick layer (roughly 1 inch) is smeared around the edges of the formicarium or in the places where the ants could possibly break out. However, care should be taken not to use too much talcum powder so that the ants cannot smear themselves with it; this can be dangerous to their health. For better protection, the talcum powder can be mixed with rubbing alcohol, for example, before use.

2. Vaseline/paraffin oil/petroleum gel: about two centimetres (roughly one inch) of this is smeared in strips around the entire formicarium as a breakout

protection. Most ants are deterred by this and turn back, as they do not want to go to the trouble of fighting their way through this material. However, there are also species that have no problem with grease and the like and are not deterred by it.

3. Fluon/PTFE ("liquid teflon"): This method is generally considered to be very effective and is often the best method, but the material is also a little more expensive. The bottles usually last quite a long time, but this method is not necessarily necessary for all ants if they can also be stopped by grease and talcum. However, for ants that are particularly eager to escape, PTFE is probably the best and most effective choice. However, care should be taken that these products can secrete gases, so they should not come into contact with the ants and should at best be applied before the ants move in.

© Franco Patrizia

The Diet

Animals are roughly divided into herbivores, carnivores and omnivores. Within these categories there are then further "specialisations". Insectivores, for example, are carnivores and leaf-eaters are herbivores.

Ants are omnivores - they can digest and use both plant and animal food.

For all species, care should be taken to provide a balanced and reasonably varied diet. Offering a variety of different foods is also important to provide the ants with a varied diet. Each food offers different macro-

and micronutrients that help to supply the body with all essential nutrients. Of course, the ants don't need to be offered new plants every day, but there should always be a good selection available so that the ants can also select a little according to their needs.

However, there is no need to worry if the entire colony does not seek out and actively consume the food, but if only some of the ants do so. The other ants will still not starve - because as we have learned before, ants have the crop (i.e., the so-called "social stomach") in which they store food in order to regurgitate it later and feed other ants with it. This "service" of food delivery not only benefits the queen, but the workers also feed each other by means of their social stomach.

In general, with all animals, one should try to offer them a diet that is close to their diet in the wild. In the wild, many ants feed to a very large extent on honeydew. This is given off by aphids and scale insects. Offering honeydew from aphids (or scale insects) in the home formicarium is therefore naturally quite difficult - not impossible, but rather inconvenient. Therefore, the most common and popular alternative is: honey water! Although honey can also be offered without prior dilution, mixing it with water makes it somewhat easier for the ants. About two thirds of the honey is mixed with one third of the water. In this way, the ants can absorb the honey better and more easily, because pure honey is very viscous and more difficult for the ants to absorb.

You should also make sure that the honey is of excellent quality. If you have an organic beekeeper nearby, this would be the best choice. In any case, care must be taken that the honey is of high quality, otherwise it is possible that there may be pesticides in the honey, which could poison the ants in the worst case.

The honey water provides the ants with plenty of carbohydrates. In addition, the ants should always be offered some fruit. Ideally, you should not always choose the same one or two types of fruit but vary them a little now and then to ensure a varied diet.

Suitable fruits, for example, are ...

... apples

... bananas

... pears

... strawberries

... kiwi

... grapes

It should be noted, however, that although the majority of ants also consume carbohydrates in the form of fruit, not all of them do. Messor ant species do not need fruit, but instead grains and seeds such as grass seeds and dandelion seeds. It is also important to ensure that the grains and seeds are of excellent organic quality.

Offering a variety of different foods is also important to provide the ants with a versatile diet. Each food offers different macro- and micronutrients that help to supply the body with all essential nutrients. Of course, the ants do not need to be offered new plants every day, but there should always be a little selection available so that the ants can also select a bit according to their needs. On the other hand, you should avoid foods that are too spicy, such as onions. These are usually not touched by the ants anyway.

Ants also need some animal protein in the form of dead insects. This is therefore carrion. The animal protein is especially important for the larvae, as they depend on more protein than the "adult" ants.

Suitable foods are, for example ...

... cockroaches (e.g., Shelfordella lateralis)

... flies (e.g., Drosophila melanogaster)

... grasshoppers

... house crickets (Acheta domesticus)

Worms, bugs and beetles, on the other hand, should not be offered to the ants. With worms there is also the danger that the digestive juices are negatively affected.

Furthermore, it is important to note that insects can in many cases have mites, which can be passed on to the ants when they are fed and in the worst-case scenario can even wipe out the entire colony. Therefore, make sure that the quality is excellent - and if in doubt, boil or deep-freeze the insects to kill any mites.

Ants, of course, do not eat as much as other larger pets. Nevertheless, care should be taken to ensure that food in the form of honey water, fruit and dead insects is always available to them. How much food should be given depends very much on the species and the colony size - so it is not possible to give a general answer here. However, over time you will notice how much or how little the ants eat and you can adjust the amounts.

Furthermore, no cereals should be fed - feeding rice, bread and the like is neither necessary nor healthy. Dairy products should also be avoided, as milk and foods made from it such as cheese, curd etc. do not belong to the species-appropriate diet of ants.

Furthermore, ants should not eat salt or industrial sugar - naturally occurring fructose is of course perfectly fine.

Also, it is important that the food is always fresh. It is therefore not enough to feed the ants only once a week, for example - the food should definitely be changed every two days. After two days at the latest, vegetable food in particular begins to ferment and is no longer safe to eat. The ants know this and will probably not touch fermented food anyway. Therefore, it is a good idea to offer enough food for about two days, then remove any leftover food and replace it with fresh food. Of course, it is also possible to feed the ants daily - but every two days should be the upper time limit.

Like all animals, ants always need access to drinking water, usually in the form of a trough. In some countries where the tap water is of good quality, this can be used. However, in many countries - and sometimes also in certain regions - this is not possible. Then it is imperative to use still bottled water. Ants are so much smaller than us that they are much more sensitive to toxins, even though they are actually quite robust animals. Water containing chlorine, for example, is a death sentence for ants.

© *Franco Patrizia*

Examples of Typical Behaviour

In this chapter we want to take a closer look at some typical behaviours of ants.

Behaviour in case of too much dryness:

As we have already learned, ants cannot cope with too much dryness and are always dependent on moisture. If it is too dry, brood rearing cannot be successful and the animals may even dry out. On the other hand, it can also happen that the brood gets mouldy if there is too much moisture or the moisture cannot be distributed over a large area. As a rule, the ants themselves take very good care of their brood and transport them to where the conditions are optimal. However, these conditions must of course be provided. If it gets too wet, the ants will transport the brood to a drier place, and if it gets too dry, they will transport the brood to a more humid place. For this reason, it is also important that the formicarium is not exposed to direct sunlight, because this can not only heat up the formicarium very quickly, but also cause it to dry out very quickly, so that in the worst case scenario the entire colony could die.

Behaviour with too much light:

Although ants (also) live on the surface of the earth, they do not like too much light - especially not when it comes to their nest. The ants' nest is always dark, no matter what the nest is made of. This, of course, also ensures the protection of the brood. If the nest is destroyed or the ants are suddenly exposed to light for some other reason, they will first bring their brood to safety by finding a dark hiding place for them.

Trophallaxis:

We have briefly discussed the subject of trophallaxis before. This is the technical term for the transfer of food and/or water between animals of a community, for example between ants of the same colony. Trophallaxis also occurs in some birds, some bats, etc., but is most common and often best developed in socially living insects such as ants. The transmission of food and/or water takes place either from mouth to mouth or from anus to mouth, depending on the species. Mouth-to-mouth transmission is called "stomodeal", while anus-to-mouth transmission is called "proctodeal". In ants, stomodeal transmission is most common, where the ant regurgitates the contents of its crop and passes them on. In this way, it not only feeds the queen, but also larvae and often other workers. The process of regurgitation from the crop is called "regurgitation". However, it should also be mentioned that not all ant species practice trophallaxis.

Fights:

While many ant species have separate female soldiers that are bigger and stronger than the normal workers and are responsible for defending the nest, all ants can fight battles - even the queens. They can defend themselves or start a fight themselves. They have various ways of doing this - the best-known way is probably the defence sting.

An "ant bite" with the defence stinger is often mistaken for an ant bite when this affects a human - but usually these injuries are not bites, but stings; similar to the stings of wasps. Many ant species still have the defence sting, but some species no longer do, as this has partially or at least largely regressed due to evolution. However, these ants still have the ability to secrete venomous secretions or at least foul-smelling secretions, which often already put an opponent to flight.

Another important fighting tool in many species are the so-called mandibles. The mandibles are the ants' mouthparts that can serve many different purposes - food can be crushed, objects can be transported and cut (e.g., leaves) and fighting can be done with the mandible. What exactly the mandibles are used for also differs from species to species, because some ants use these tools e.g., mainly for cutting up objects (leaf-cutting ants like Acromyrmex or Atta), others e.g. mainly for hunting prey (predatory species like Myrmecia). However, the ants of the Atta genus also use the mandible for fighting - as you can see, this often differs between species.

Transport:

It is no myth that ants are incredibly strong when you compare their strength to their own weight. Depending on the species, they can actually carry 30 to 40 times their own body weight, making them some of the strongest creatures around. They often carry loads not only alone, but in teams to be able to handle an even greater load. Ants do not only transport liquids or food in their social stomach (crop), the contents of which they can later regurgitate and pass on to other ants and larvae. They also carry them by means of their grasping tools (mandibles). The ants sometimes also carry each other. In addition, in many species there is also the so-called tandem run, in which one ant induces another ant to "come along", for example because it has discovered food in a certain place or because it wants to show it something else. The tandem run goes hand in hand with the recruitment behaviour (see below), because here the two ants keep constant physical contact while the following ant follows the leading ant to a previously unknown destination, for example to the new food source. The following ant keeps constant contact with the leading ant through its antennae by keeping contact with its hind legs or gaster while following. If the connection between the two ants is disturbed, the leading ant can lead the following ant back to it by means of pheromones until contact is re-established - but if the connection is disturbed several times or too deeply, the ants usually break off the tandem run and return to their nest.

Recruitment:

The tandem run already described above is considered a type of recruitment, but only one other ant is recruited. The ant that has discovered something or wants to lead its comrades to a certain place for another reason can also recruit several ants at once. However, this is then no longer done by means of a tandem run, but by means of so-called group recruitment, i.e., the recruitment of a larger group. Since the tandem run would not be very efficient with so many ants (usually up to ten ants), the leading ant lays a scent trail instead, which the following ants can use to follow it to the respective destination. In addition, so-called mass recruitment is also possible if a particularly large number of ants or even the whole colony has to move. In this case, a scent trail is also laid, but it usually has to be reinforced - this scent trail is called an "ant trail" because the ants follow it like a road and thus find their way to the destination.

Swarm intelligence:

Swarm intelligence is the collective intelligence of an entire ant group or ant colony. An ant alone is not very clever and will never survive as a lone fighter - it absolutely needs its conspecifics, no matter what activity it is doing. In a colony, all ants have certain tasks and duties, they work strongly in a team and call on their comrades for help when they have discovered a new food source, a defence case arises or the like. On its own, a single ant would hardly accomplish anything and therefore cannot really be called intelligent or particularly capable on its own, as it is only strong in a team. As a team, ants are capable of fascinating activities and establish the most elaborate and sometimes complicated structures and organisations. This is reflected in the complexity that many ants' nests have, depending on the species. But ants only achieve all this in a team - i.e., in a swarm - and not alone; hence this is called "swarm intelligence".

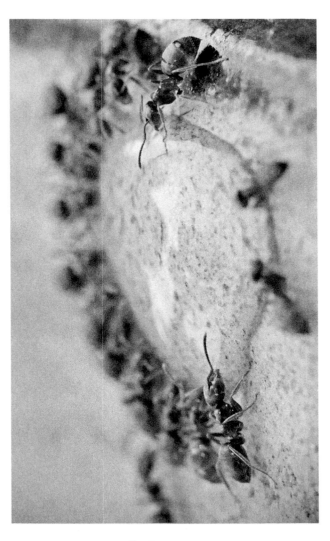

© *Gamagapix*

Hibernation

During hibernation, many animals sleep deeply and soundly for several weeks, whereas in ant hibernation (or reptile hibernation) there is usually only a period of rest during which the body regenerates and greatly reduces its bodily functions. Hibernation is not only practised by insects, but also by many reptiles, and is important for long-lasting health for most animals.

Many ant species have their home in very warm areas, often in tropical rainforests, and they do not need to hibernate in areas where temperatures are always warm. However, there are also many species that live on continents or in regions where it gets cold in the winter months. The ants concerned had to adapt to this. However, the vast majority of ants are cold-blooded - just like reptiles. This means that the animals do not regulate their body temperature themselves (like mammals), but that the body temperature is adapted to the ambient temperature. In cold periods, the body functions are therefore very much reduced.

Many keepers do not want to keep a species of ant that goes into hibernation because they want to be able to observe the ants all year round. This is quite understandable, as hibernation should be between four and six months long, depending on the species. However, it is not an alternative to choose Central European or Mediterranean ant species and then deprive them of their winter rest. Instead, one could choose a species that originates from tropical areas and therefore naturally does not hibernate. Camponotus nicobarensis, for example, are among these species that do not require hibernation. A beginner is nevertheless well advised to choose an ant species that does hibernate but is uncomplicated to handle.

The hibernation period for Central European ant species should begin around September or October. As it is usually very cold in Central Europe for a long time, hibernation for these species (e.g., for the ever-popular and uncomplicated Lasius niger) even lasts around half a year. These species therefore ideally spend the period from the beginning of October to the end of March in hibernation. This may seem like a very long time, but the ants need this period of hibernation to fully recover and regenerate - so to speak, to be able to "hit the ground running" again in spring and summer.

If, on the other hand, you decide to keep an ant species that originates from Mediterranean regions, you should also have a hibernation period, but this does not last quite as long, but only about four months. With these species, for example, hibernation can be started at the beginning of November and ended at the end of February.

The most important thing during hibernation is that the ants do not dry out! Sometimes ants do not survive hibernation and unfortunately die - and dehydration is almost always the reason! Of course, the ants should not "swim" in water, because they can also drown, especially during hibernation. But wet kitchen paper, for example, is very good for keeping the ant and the environment moist during hibernation. Spray bottles are also very suitable for moistening, which atomise the water evenly.

So now the question arises at what temperature the ants should be "stored" in winter. In this respect, it can be stated that most ant species become active again at a temperature of above 10°C (50°F). Therefore, during hibernation, the ambient temperature should be less than 10°C (50°F). However, this temperature should not drop under 1°C (33°F), because we don't want our ants to freeze! A temperature of around 5°C (40°F) is therefore ideal for most species.

For this reason, many ant keepers like to keep their ants in the fridge for the winter. The fridge temperature can of course be set individually, but as a rule, most fridges have a temperature of around 5°C to 6°C (roughly 40°F). The fridge is therefore an ideal environment for the ants during hibernation!

Another option is to house the ants on the balcony, in the garden, in the garage, in the cellar or similar cold places. Here, of course, the temperature is more difficult or impossible to influence. If the ants spend the winter outside, they should always be protected from sudden changes in the weather. In any case, they need protection against frost so that they do not freeze. Direct sunlight should also be avoided.

Cold places such as garages or cellars are easier to influence in terms of temperature and there the ants do not need to be protected from the sun. However, it is questionable whether the temperature in the cellar or garage is already below 10°C (50°F) in October/November. This also depends very much on where you live. In many areas of Europe and America it is still much warmer than 10°C / 50°F at this time.

If an ant species that would actually go into hibernation in the wild does not go into hibernation, this can sometimes have serious consequences. These consequences are not always immediately recognisable and it is also possible that they only occur after a few years. Often there is no clear cause for these problems and it is quite possible that they are due to the lack of hibernation. Not all of these problems occur in all colonies; one can also be "lucky". But to keep the colony healthy and lively in the long run, hibernation should not be denied.

Possible problems include various changes within the colony. In the worst case scenario, the entire colony may slowly die off, even if otherwise good husbandry conditions are ensured.

The other problems that occur quite frequently in the absence of hibernation are almost all related to reproduction. For example, it is possible that brood rearing is reduced overall or no longer happens regularly. Furthermore, it can happen that no or hardly any sexual development takes place or that the larvae increasingly die.

By the way, many keepers are surprised in the autumn season that their ants eat less, are no longer as active as before and/or that no more eggs are laid. Many keepers are right to worry whether the colony is ill or whether the housing conditions are not right. In most cases, however, this behaviour is due to the fact that the ants are preparing for their natural hibernation and are already slowly reducing their activities. Even if the ants live permanently at home in the formicarium, they usually still have instinctively internalised their natural rhythm of life or annual rhythm, because this has developed over thousands of years as the ants slowly adapted to their respective homes in the wild.

Of course, this rhythm can fluctuate somewhat and does not always resemble the rhythm of wild ants, since ants as pets live differently than their conspecifics in the wild - ants living at home, for example, do not have to "worry" about finding food and already live in spring under higher temperatures than ants outside.

Ants sense when winter hibernation is approaching, so they empty their gut and crop beforehand. As we already know, the crop is a stomach in which the ant "stores" food and regurgitates it when it is needed. In this way, the ant can store food and feed it to other workers, the queen and the larvae, should this become necessary. For this reason, the crop is also called a "social stomach".

The ant's body fluids are thickened and the freezing point of these fluids is reduced. The glycerine content and the salt content increase. In this way, the ants become less sensitive to the cold temperatures and many ants can even survive sub-zero temperatures without freezing to death and dying of frostbite -

nevertheless, one should not try this in order not to expose the ants to unnecessary risk.

© *Leona 2013*

Diseases and Dangers

In this chapter, we will take a closer look at some diseases and health hazards - first we will look at diseases that can affect the animals, as well as hazards for the ants. Finally, we will look at some of the dangers to humans that ants may pose.

Oxygen, carbon dioxide & bad air quality

Good ventilation of the ant home is essential to prevent or at least contain mould and the spread of disease. Of course, ants rely on adequate humidity, but if the ant home doesn't get fresh air, food will start to mould much faster and pathogens can spread more easily. Regular fresh air is also important to provide the ants with enough oxygen. Otherwise, the CO_2 level can rise too high and in the worst case even cause the death of the ants, as they could suffocate due to the lack of oxygen. The CO_2 is produced naturally by the ants' respiration, because ants - like us humans - breathe in oxygen and breathe out CO_2. In addition, mould, for example, also increases the CO_2 content.

Parasites

Parasites are basically divided into ectoparasites and endoparasites. Ectoparasites are "external living" parasites, for example mites on the skin. Endoparasites are "internal" parasites.

Artificially created habitats - for example, in formicariums - cause an infestation to intensify quite quickly if it is not recognised and treated at an early stage, because there is not too much space available in the formicarium. How strong or weak the parasite infestation is often also strongly depends on the living conditions. Poor housing conditions weaken the animals' immune system and thus their defences.

The most common ectoparasites in ants, i.e. parasites that live outside the animal's body, are definitely mites. Mites are not always to be seen as a disease, because mites occur naturally throughout our environment. Whether mites are harmful depends partly on the species and partly on how large the mite infestation is.

The most common endoparasites in ants, i.e. parasites that live inside the ants' bodies, are tapeworms and threadworms, for example. In case of an infestation, the gaster often swells considerably.

Fungal infestation

Similar to parasites, fungi can also occur either outside the ant's body or inside it. For example, an external and quite common fungus in ants is the Aegeritella fungus - this is quite visible. Another fungus that specifically affects Myrmica ant species is the Rickia wasmannii fungus. In addition, there are some fungi that spread in the ant body itself - first and foremost the Beauveria bassiana fungus, which specifically affects queens and can even cause their death. Another fungus that specifically affects ants belonging to the Formica genus is the Pandora myrmecophaga fungus.

Ant bites

Ant stings are very often confused with ant bites. It is true that ants can bite by means of their mandibles, but the most common injuries are ant "bites" with the defence sting and not actual bites. Not all ant species still have a defence sting and in some it is atrophied or no longer present. As a rule, ant bites are harmless to most people, although there are some specimens that can cause great pain or, in the worst case, even kill - for example, the red fire ant. However, these poisonous species are not usually kept as pets anyway. Furthermore, it is also crucial how "sensitive" the respective person reacts to the ant venom, because not everyone reacts to ant stings in the same way. Unfortunately, people also die again and again from wasp stings, although the majority of people can ward off the venom of a wasp rather well. If allergies to wasp stings, for example, are already known, keeping a potentially stinging ant species should therefore be avoided in any case, as the venoms are quite similar. The same applies to bee stings.

Invasive ants

Every animal species has a natural habitat, which can
sometimes be larger and sometimes smaller. The
animal species has adapted to this habitat over a long
period of time, is accustomed to the environmental
conditions and usually also has natural counterparts to
naturally maintain the balance in the animal kingdom.
However, if a species invades and spreads into a new
habitat, and if, in addition, its reproduction is not
regulated by parasites, predators or other counterparts,
it is an invasive species. Simply put, the natural balance
is no longer there. In the worst case, originally native
species may be displaced by the invasive species and
biodiversity may suffer from the invasion. Invasive ant
species are usually spread to new areas by travellers
and/or commodity traders. Once an invasive ant
species has established itself in the new area, it is very
difficult or impossible to reverse this, also because the
ants spread so quickly and are not easy to "catch" due
to their size. There are some areas, for example in the
USA, where hardly any other ant species can be found,
apart from the invasive species. In many cases, these
are the species Linepithema humile and Solenopsis

invicta. A total of about twenty different invasive ant species are known, for example also Nylanderia pubens (invasive in Mexico, USA, etc.), Myrmica ruba (invasive in the USA and Canada), Monomorium floricola (invasive in numerous African and European countries, but also on the Australian and American continent), etc.

© *Roman Grac - Diego Torres*

Dear reader: For independent authors, product reviews are the basis for the success of a book. Therefore, we depend on your reviews. This not only helps the authors, but of course also future readers and the animals! Therefore, I would be extremely grateful for a little review on this book. Thank you very much.

I wish you all the best, much joy with your ants and the best of health!

© Alexas Fotos

Legal Notice

Author: Alina Daria Djavidrad

Contact: Wahlerstraße 1, 40472 Düsseldorf, Germany

1st edition (2021)

Room for Notes

Printed in Great Britain
by Amazon